LIFE WITHOUT ANIMALS

WHAT IF SEA URCHINS DISAPPEARED?

By Theresa Emminizer

Gareth Stevens
PUBLISHING

Please visit our website, www.garethstevens.com. For a free color catalog of all our high-quality books, call toll free 1-800-542-2595 or fax 1-877-542-2596.

Library of Congress Cataloging-in-Publication Data

Names: Emminizer, Theresa, author.
Title: What if sea urchins disappeared? / Theresa Emminizer.
Description: New York : Gareth Stevens, [2020] | Series: Life without animals | Includes index.
Identifiers: LCCN 2019002459| ISBN 9781538238264 (paperback) | ISBN 9781538238288 (library bound) | ISBN 9781538238271 (6 pack)
Subjects: LCSH: Sea urchins–Conservation–Juvenile literature. | Endangered species–Juvenile literature.
Classification: LCC QL384.E2 E46 2020 | DDC 593.9/5–dc23
LC record available at https://lccn.loc.gov/2019002459

Published in 2020 by
Gareth Stevens Publishing
111 East 14th Street, Suite 349
New York, NY 10003

Designer: Laura Bowen
Editor: Theresa Emminizer

Photo credits: cover, p. 1 NatalieJean/Shutterstock.com; pp. 3-24 (series art) De-V/Shutterstock.com; p. 5 William Lermond/Shutterstock.com; p. 7 ratchaneewarn sumitrakij/Shutterstock.com; p. 9 PurMoon/Shutterstock.com; p. 11 Jérémie LeBlond-Fontaine/Moment/Getty Images; p. 13 Nicole Helgason/Shutterstock.com; p. Mr.anaked/Shutterstock.com; p. 17 David Courtenay/Oxford Scientific; p. 19 Ralph A. Clevenger/Corbis/Getty Images; p. 21 Vstock LLC/VStock/Getty Images.

Printed in the United States of America

CPSIA compliance information: Batch #CS19GS: For further information contact Gareth Stevens, New York, New York at 1-800-542-2595.

CONTENTS

Boldface words appear in the glossary.

What Are Sea Urchins?

Sea urchins are echinoderms, a type of **invertebrate** ocean animal. They have round bodies, covered in **spines**. There are hundreds of species, or kinds, of sea urchins. They are an important part of ocean **ecosystems**. What would happen if sea urchins disappeared?

Where Do They Live?

Sea urchins live in saltwater. They can be found in all oceans. Different species live in different areas. They may live in warm or cold waters. They may be black, blue, brown, green, yellow, or red in color.

What Do They Eat?

Sea urchins are omnivorous. That means they are both plant and meat eaters. They can often be found in **coral reefs**, rock pools, and sea grass beds searching for food. Their main foods are **algae** and seaweed. They also eat dead animals, including other urchins!

Why Are They Important?

By eating algae, sea urchins help keep ocean **habitats** healthy. They also supply food to the habitat. Sea urchins are an important food for many other marine, or ocean, species. Sea otters, starfish, and sea gulls hunt sea urchins. People eat them, too!

An Indicator Species

Sea urchins are an "indicator species." That means that by looking at sea urchins, people are able to learn about the health of the whole ecosystem. If sea urchins are doing well, it usually means that the water is clean.

marine biologist studying sea urchins

What Harms Urchins?

Pollution can make sea urchins sick and even kill them. Pollution is when waste, **chemicals**, and other harmful things dirty the earth or ocean. Oil spills are a kind of pollution that can wipe out large groups of sea urchins.

What Could Happen?

If sea urchins disappeared, species that eat them, such as sea otters, could also disappear. Sea otters are a keystone species. That means many other species need them to **survive**. Without sea urchins to feed sea otters, the ecosystem could fall apart.

Without sea urchins to keep them in check, algae and kelp could grow out of control. Too much plant growth can actually pollute the water! Algae can let out harmful gases and cut off **oxygen**, killing fish.

You Can Help!

What can you do to help sea urchins? Keeping beaches and oceans clean will help keep sea urchins safe. Even if you don't live near the ocean, you can do your part by cutting down the amount of trash you make.

GLOSSARY

algae: plantlike living things that are mostly found in water

chemical: matter that can be mixed with other matter to cause changes

coral reef: underwater mound made up of the hard parts of tiny sea animals

ecosystem: all the living things in an area

habitat: the natural place where an animal or plant lives

invertebrate: an animal without a backbone

oxygen: a colorless, odorless gas that many animals, including people, need to breathe

spine: a stiff, pointed part growing from an animal

survive: to live through something

FOR MORE INFORMATION

BOOKS

Rajczak, Michael. *Things That Sting: Sea Urchins.* New York, NY: Gareth Stevens Publishing, 2015.

Rake, Jody S. *Faceless, Spineless, and Brainless Ocean Animals: Sea Urchins.* Mankato, MN: Capstone Press, 2016.

WEBSITES

Aquarium of the Pacific
aquariumofpacific.org/onlinelearningcenter/species/red_sea_urchin
Read more fun facts about sea urchins.

DK Find Out!
dkfindout.com/uk/animals-and-nature/starfish-sea-urchins-and-sea-cucumbers/sea-urchins/
Learn more about sea urchins' bodies and how they live.

Publisher's note to educators and parents: Our editors have carefully reviewed these websites to ensure that they are suitable for students. Many websites change frequently, however, and we cannot guarantee that a site's future contents will continue to meet our high standards of quality and educational value. Be advised that students should be closely supervised whenever they access the internet.

INDEX